BANGLADESH

LETTERS FROM AROUND THE WORLD

David Cumming

Photographs by Howard Davies

CHERRYTREE BOOKS

Titles in this series

BANGLADESH • BRAZIL • CHINA • FRANCE • INDIA • ITALY • JAMAICA • JAPAN • KENYA • SPAIN

A Cherrytree Book

Conceived and produced by

Nutshell
MEDIA

Intergen House
65-67 Western Road
Hove BN3 2JQ, UK
www.nutshellmedialtd.co.uk

First published in 2003 by
Evans Brothers Ltd
2A Portman Mansions
Chiltern Street
London W1U 6NR

VISIT OUR WEBSITE www.evansbooks.co.uk

© Copyright Evans Brothers 2003

Editor: Katie Orchard
Designer: Tim Mayer
Map artwork: Encompass Graphics Ltd
All other artwork: Tim Mayer
Geography consultant: Jeff Stanfield, Geography
   Inspector for Ofsted
Literacy consultant: Anne Spiring

All photographs were taken by Howard Davies.

Printed in Hong Kong.

Acknowledgements
The photographer would like to thank the following for
their help: the Talukder family; the imam of Lalkhatongi
Mosque, the teachers and pupils at Lalkhatongi School,
Tufayel Ahmed, Alam Gil, Salim Malik and Vinod Mashru.

British Library Cataloguing in Publication Data
Cumming, David
   Bangladesh – (Letters from around the world)
   1. Bangladesh – Social conditions – Juvenile literature
   2. Bangladesh – Social life and customs – Juvenile
   literature
   I. Title
   954.9'2'05

ISBN 1 84234 146 4

Cover: Sabrina stands with her younger sister Hassena
   (left) and her friend Khaleda (right) outside her home.
Title page: Sabrina on her way to school.
This page: Tea pickers at a tea plantation near Sylhet.
Contents page: Sabrina's dad ploughs a rice field.
Glossary: Collecting water from a pump.
Further information page: Sabrina and Hassena do their
   homework outside their house.
Index: Street traders sell their wares in Lalkhatongi.

Contents

My Country

Monday, 15 November

Talukder
c/o Main Post Office
Sylhet
Bangladesh

Dear Alex,

Asalam walekum! (This means 'hello' in Bangla, my language.)

My name is Sabrina Talukder and I'm 8 years old. I live in Lalkhatongi, a village in north-east Bangladesh. I have four brothers and three sisters. Do you have a big family, too?

Let me know if I can help with your school projects on Bangladesh.

From
Sabrina ↗

Here I am (in the orange top) with Dad (in white), Mum (in green and red), and some of my brothers and sisters.

Bangladesh is a small country next to India. Dhaka is the capital and also the biggest city. About 132 million people live in Bangladesh.

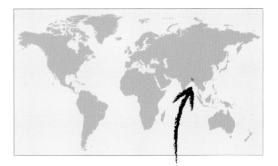

Bangladesh's place in the world.

INDIA

INDIA

KHASI HILLS

Sylhet   Shahparan
Lalkhatongi

Brahmaputra (Jamuna)

Meghna

Ganges (Padma)

INDIA

DHAKA

BANGLADESH

N

INDIA

Khulna

CHITTAGONG HILLS

Chittagong

Keokradong
1,230m △

BAY OF
BENGAL

MYANMAR
(BURMA)

The name 'Bangladesh' means 'land of the Bangla-speaking people'.

0   50   100   150   200 kilometres

0   50   100 miles

Bangladesh has few cities. Most people live in villages. About 1,000 people live in Lalkhatongi. The nearest town is Sylhet, about 10 kilometres away. Sabrina's parents go to Sylhet to collect their mail from the post office.

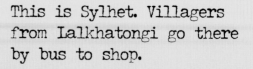

This is Sylhet. Villagers from Lalkhatongi go there by bus to shop.

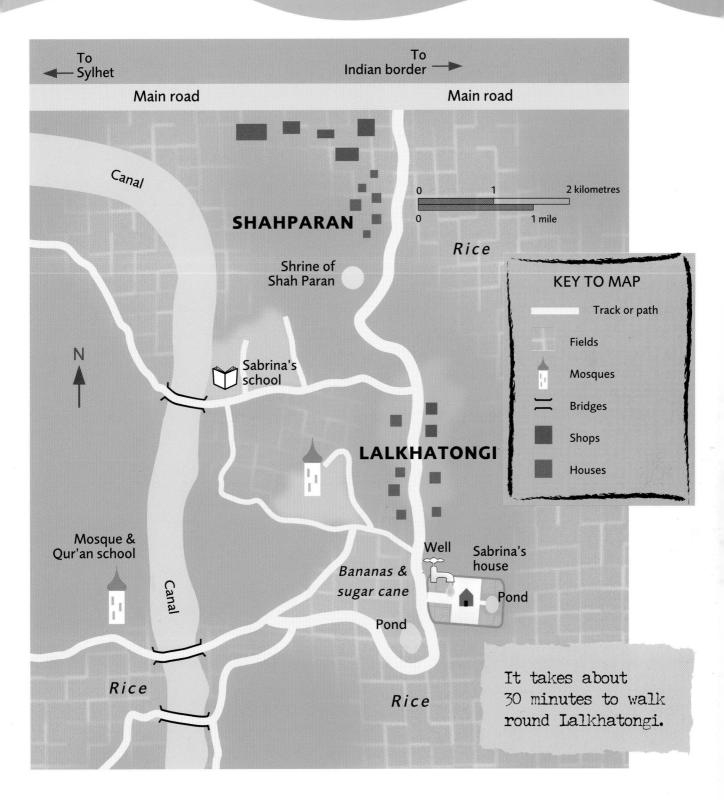

To
← To Sylhet

To
Indian border →

Main road   Main road

Canal

SHAHPARAN

Rice

Shrine of
Shah Paran

0   1   2 kilometres
0   1 mile

N ↑

Sabrina's
school

LALKHATONGI

Mosque &
Qur'an school

Canal

Well   Sabrina's
house

Bananas &
sugar cane

Pond

Pond

Rice   Rice

KEY TO MAP

Track or path
Fields
Mosques
Bridges
Shops
Houses

It takes about
30 minutes to walk
round Lalkhatongi.

There are two small grocery shops near Sabrina's
home. The people in Lalkhatongi grow most of
their own food on small plots of land.

Landscape and Weather

Most of Bangladesh is very flat and low. Many rivers cross the country on their way to the sea. In Lalkhatongi the flat land is used to grow rice. In the hills around Sylhet, there are tea plantations.

Rice grows quickly in Lalkhatongi's hot and wet climate.

In Bangladesh, between October and February it is usually dry and no hotter than 20°C. From March to September the temperature can reach as high as 35°C and there is a lot of rain. This is called the monsoon season. Often there is too much rain and the rivers flood.

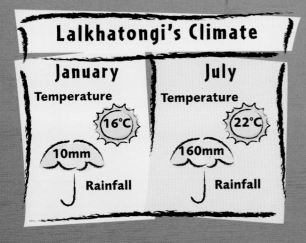

Lalkhatongi's Climate

January

Temperature

16°C

10mm

Rainfall

July

Temperature

22°C

160mm

Rainfall

Stilts keep these houses
dry when the **river floods**
during the monsoon months.

At Home

Sabrina and her family live in a small house. It has a tin roof and the walls are made of straw. Sabrina likes the sound of the monsoon rain on the roof. It makes her sleepy.

Sabrina stands by the cow shed and barn in front of the entrance to her home.

There are four rooms – two bedrooms, a living room and a kitchen. Sabrina shares one of the bedrooms with all her brothers and sisters.

Sabrina usually does her homework at a desk in the bedroom.

Sabrina's house does not have running water. Every day Sabrina's mum collects clean water for drinking and cooking from a pump outside the house.

Sometimes Sabrina helps her mum collect drinking water from the pump.

One of Sabrina's jobs is to collect water from the pond for washing.

Sabrina brings home one of the cows from the field.

Sabrina's family owns two cows and a goat. The animals live in the cow shed. There is also a garden with a pond. The pond water is not clean enough to drink, but the family uses it to wash clothes and to water the garden.

Wednesday, 12 December

Talukder
c/o Main Post Office
Sylhet
Bangladesh

Dear Alex,

Thanks for your letter. You're right – we don't have gas or electricity for cooking. We use dung instead. We collect it from the cow shed. Then we mould it on to sticks and leave them out to dry in the sun. The dung burns easily and gives out lots of heat. Having the fuel on sticks means that it is easy to move the heat to where it is needed.

From
Sabrina

Sometimes I help Mum put dung on sticks to use in the fire.

Food and Mealtimes

The Talukders have little money, so their food is nearly always the same. The family has breakfast after getting up at 6 a.m. Breakfast is usually tea and biscuits or bread.

For lunch and dinner they eat curried vegetables and *dhal* (spicy lentils), with rice and *chapattis* (flat bread).

Sabrina's dad does most of the shopping. He buys garlic in one of the village grocery shops.

Sabrina's family rarely eats meat because it is expensive. They never eat pork because it is not allowed by their religion, Islam. Sometimes the Talukders eat prawns or fish. The children catch them in the canal nearby.

People in Bangladesh always eat with their right hand.

Sabrina's family grows their
own fruit and vegetables,
such as bananas, spinach,
beans, onions and potatoes.
They buy other things from
one of the village shops.

Sabrina waters
the vegetables
in the garden.

Tuesday, 18 January

Talukder
c/o Main Post Office
Sylhet
Bangladesh

Hi Alex,

Here's the Bangladeshi recipe I promised you. Why don't you make some *dhal*?

You will need: 1 tablespoon oil, 1 chopped onion, 2 crushed garlic cloves, 1 teaspoon cumin seeds, 1 teaspoon turmeric, 175g lentils, 600ml water, 1 tablespoon chopped fresh coriander, salt and pepper to taste.

1. Heat the oil in a saucepan. Add the onion and fry until soft.
2. Add the garlic, cumin and turmeric, and fry for 1 minute.
3. Add the lentils and water, and bring to the boil. Cover the pan and simmer for 20 minutes, stirring occasionally.
4. Add the coriander, salt and pepper.

Let me know what you think!

From
Sabrina

I'm putting the *dhal* on some vegetables for dinner.

School Day

Sabrina goes to a primary school in Lalkhatongi. Like most schools in Bangladesh it is a state school, so it is free. Sabrina always walks there and back.

Sabrina walks to school with some of her classmates. It takes her twenty minutes.

Sabrina waits outside her classroom for lessons to begin.

The school is small and there are only two teachers. There is not enough room for all the village children to go there at the same time. Half of them go in the morning and the other half go in the afternoon.

Sabrina practises reading Bangla, the language of Bangladesh.

Sabrina's classes are in the afternoon, from 12.30 p.m. to 3.30 p.m. She learns Bangla, maths, English and religious studies.

Posters at school show letters in English and Bangla.

Sabrina goes to school from Saturday to Thursday. She gets homework every day.

There is no school on Friday, Islam's holy day. Most days, Sabrina also has lessons on Islam at the mosque.

Sabrina helps her little sister with her English homework.

Thursday, 23 February

Talukder
c/o Main Post Office
Sylhet
Bangladesh

Dear Alex,

Do you like school? I love it, but I'm not very good at maths!

As well as school, I have classes at my mosque. I go there every morning at 7 a.m. The imam (the priest) teaches us about Islam. We also read a bit from the Qur'an, our holy book, and talk about it. The lesson usually lasts an hour.

Do you have any extra lessons?

From

Sabrina

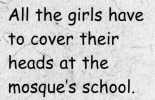

All the girls have to cover their heads at the mosque's school.

Off to Work

Sabrina's dad works for a farmer, looking after his rice fields. The farmer does not pay him. Instead Mr Talukder gets half the harvest. He keeps some of it and sells the rest. Sabrina's mum stays at home to look after the house and the children.

Sabrina's dad ploughs a field with the help of his two cows.

Tea pickers work at a plantation near Sylhet.

Most Bangladeshis are farmers. As well as rice and tea, they grow sugar cane and jute. There are big factories in major cities such as Dhaka and Chittagong. They make clothes and leather.

The bricks made in this small factory in Sylhet will be used to build new homes.

Free Time

Few of Sabrina's friends have toys bought for them. They make their own from bits and pieces that people have thrown away.

These village children are taking turns riding in a cart they have made.

Sabrina and her friends play a skipping game.

With so many brothers and sisters, Sabrina can always find enough people to play blind man's buff.

Sabrina and her friends usually make up games or play hide-and-seek and tag. They spend a lot of time outside because it is always warm. Only the monsoon makes them stay indoors.

Most people in Bangladesh have very little free time. On Fridays Sabrina often visits her grandmother. She lives in a village about an hour's walk away.

Religion and Festivals

Men praying at a mosque on a Friday.

The main religion in Bangladesh is Islam. There are also some Hindus and a small number of Buddhists and Christians.

One of the most important Muslim festivals is Ramadan. During Ramadan Muslims do not eat or drink during the day.

These boys are studying the Qur'an, Islam's holy book.

Saturday, 8 March

Talukder
c/o Main Post Office
Sylhet
Bangladesh

Dear Alex,

It's been really exciting here today. We went to our neighbouring village, Shahparan. The village is named after Shah Paran, a holy man who is buried there. Every day, hundreds of Muslims come from all over Bangladesh to visit his shrine.

Today the colourful covers over the shrine were blessed and replaced. This happens only once a year. We always go to see the celebrations – it's great fun!

From

Sabrina

Changing the covers of the shrine of Shah Paran.

Fact File

Capital city: The capital of Bangladesh is Dhaka. It has a population of 8 million.

Other major cities: Chittagong and Khulna.

History: Bangladesh was once part of India. It was known then as East Bengal. In 1947 East Bengal became East Pakistan, part of the new country of Pakistan. In 1971 East Pakistan fought to leave Pakistan and became Bangladesh.

Size: 144,000km^2.

Population: 132 million.

Flag: The flag of Bangladesh is dark green with a red circle in the middle. The green stands for the countryside and for the 'newness' of Bangladesh. It is also the colour of Islam. The red stands for the rising sun and also for all the blood spilt in the war in 1971.

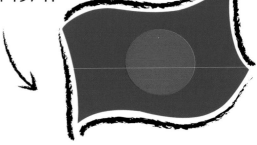

Currency: Taka (divided into paise). 1 taka = 100 paise.

Main industries: The main industries in Bangladesh make clothes, jute, leather and paper for newspapers.

Highest point: Keokradong (1,230m). More than 75 per cent of the land in Bangladesh is less than 10m above the sea.

Longest rivers: Ganges (2,510km) and Brahmaputra (2,900km). The Brahmaputra starts in China and the Ganges starts in India. When the Brahmaputra enters Bangladesh its name changes to the River Jamuna. After the Jamuna meets the Ganges, the river is renamed the Padma.

Languages: Bangla (Bengali) and English.

Stamps: Bangladeshi stamps usually show important buildings and people, and daily life in the country.

Main religions: About 83 per cent of people in Bangladesh are Muslims and 16 per cent are Hindus. There are also some Buddhists and Christians.

Main festivals: Ramadan and Id-ul-Fitr (a celebration that comes at the end of the month of Ramadan) are some of the important festivals in Islam. Diwali (the festival of lights) is the biggest celebration in the Hindu calendar.

Glossary

chapatti Circular flat bread like a thick pancake.

curried Flavoured with spices, such as chilli and cumin.

dhal A dish made with lentils, onion and spices.

harvest The time when farmers gather the crops they have grown.

Id-ul-Fitr A Muslim festival at the end of the month of Ramadan.

jute A plant used to make ropes and sacks.

monsoon The name given to the wind that blows over Bangladesh from the Indian Ocean. It brings a lot of rain.

mosque The place where Muslims worship.

Muslims People who follow the religion of Islam.

plantation A large farm where just one crop is grown to be sold abroad.

Qur'an The holy book of Islam.

Ramadan The ninth month in the Muslim year during which Muslims do not eat or drink between sunrise and sunset.

shrine A sacred place. It can be a building, or a special area inside a home.

state school A school that is paid for by the government.

stilts Poles that raise buildings off the ground to stop them flooding.

Further Information

Information books:

Continents: Asia by Leila Merrell Foster (Heinemann, 2002)

In the Eye of the Storm: Life on an Island in Bangladesh by Lucy Marcovitch (ActionAid, 2000)

Keystones: Muslim Mosque by Umar Hegedus (A & C Black, 2000)

Fiction:

Folk Tales of Bangladesh by P. C. Roy Chaudhury (Macmillan, 1990)

Stories from Asia – India, Pakistan and Bangladesh edited by Madhu Bhinda (Longman, 1992)

Resource packs:

A Bangladesh Photopack by Urszula Robinson (Learning Design, 1997)

Wake up World! by Beatrice Hollyer (Frances Lincoln/Oxfam, 1999)

Websites:

CIA World Factbook
www.cia.gov/cia/publications/factbook/
Facts and figures about Bangladesh and other countries.

Oxfam
www.oxfam.org.uk/campaign/
This website has stories about low-paid workers in the clothing industry in Bangladesh.

Virtual Bangladesh
www.virtualbangladesh.com/
Lots of information about Bangladesh, with useful links to other sites.

Index